To Chris
with love
Bill

1973

D1558575

MAINE

William Berchen

HOUGHTON MIFFLIN COMPANY BOSTON 1973

To Ursula, who worked so hard to make it possible.

Acknowledgements "Perfection" from CANTICO: *A Selection* by Jorge Guellén, and edited by
Norman Thomas diGiovanni. Translated from the original by Barbara Howes.
Copyright ©1965 by Jorge Guellén & Norman Thomas diGiovanni.
Reprinted by permission of Atlantic-Little, Brown.
I am indebted to Chris Berchen, Anita McClellan, and Joseph and Carole
Keating for editorial assistance. I am especially grateful to my editor Austin
Olney for his guidance and great patience. Finally, my gratitude to the people of
Maine whose unfailing courtesy made it all easier.

First published in 1973 by Houghton Mifflin Company, Boston, Mass. 02107
Library of Congress catalog number 72-9592
SBN 0-395-15457-X
Printed and bound in Italy by Mondadori Editore, Verona.

A Maine Village and the Law of Diminishing Returns

A pox on the travel writer who discovers an unspoiled paradise and then sells the dream for a mess of pottage!

There it is, the beaches are uncrowded, the air is soft, warm, and pollution free, the natives are friendly and ungrasping (not having learned our ways yet). Sand fleas, ticks, mosquitoes, flies, centipedes, scorpions, snakes, and red ants are non-existent, or are at a minimum. Dengue fever and malaria are unheard of, and, best of all, everything is clean and cheap. Why does our writer give away the secret, give away that which only when kept secret remains paradise? O, shades of Puerto Vallarta! Now people will come in droves. Up planes, up hotels, up prices, and then the coup de grâce: they'll make a movie there. Why, with so little left untouched by mass travel, does he mark the way for invasion? The money for the article is little enough and soon gone. Does he perchance wallow in misguided humanitarianism and feel that the Hilton culture will give the ultimate benefits of its marvels to the land and people? Or did he do it for his writer's ego, a thing in this case of the basest value?

So, to those who have paid cold cash for this book, even for you I'll not reveal the name of this little place I found in Maine. There is an untagged picture of it in the book, and if you can track it down you deserve the delight of discovery. I am sure after all the trouble you took that you will not abuse it.

Let me tell you about this remnant of nineteenth-century America. It lies in one of those thousands of inlets that form the coast of Maine, a self-contained New England village sitting in miraculous space and quiet because it has been bypassed by progress. (Beware of progress, for it may only be the development of an error, said Cocteau.) The village center, not yet gutted for a parking lot, its definition in space unswamped by eateries, gas stations, car emporia, and mammoth dispensers of plastic trash. Not that the New England village should be preserved in amber to become a museum piece, thus losing its truth by being displaced from the environment and becoming encased and sterile. Here, my village is being lived in, cared for, and, whether by accident or purposeful resistance, is kept from being trampled on. Often, though, I have the desperate thought that the real reason most things are left unspoiled is because we simply haven't gotten to them yet, having been busy elsewhere.

How do you find this village? You must be a shunpiking, byway wanderer. If you are, you will discover it, or one like it. There are some left. It was a right day in September for me to discover it. There was a sharp undercurrent in the air, and the hot sun was only occasionally cooled by a cloud. I came to the top of a rise on which sat a few of those large New England farm-houses, beautifully crafted and full of high-ceilinged rooms impossible to heat in winter, but lovely and cool in summer: homes built with a generosity of space that in these days of lumber-foot-cost analysis is incredible.

From this rise looking across a causeway connecting the shores of the inlet you see it: a beautiful collection of shelters for man designed with a natural feel for rightness. Its variety enclosed in a harmony of overall design, this village is a grouping of buildings whose beauty is partly dependent on how it sits in space, born as it was to the agrarian America of open fields broken by stone walls and wood copse. Here it is, a small miracle — church, common, a few dozen houses, post office and grange hall — seemingly unmarked and uninvaded by a branch of one of Maine's large traffic arteries fifteen minutes away by car.

It is near noon now, and time for lunch on the steps of the grange hall, a generous white building with a country road forking off to one side of it, and a view of the church, common, and inlet from the steps that is almost a religious experience.

There in the sun, its heat magnified by the white clapboard, one of the better hours of my existence passes. A car goes by only every ten minutes or so. The warmth and quiet settle on me. By quiet I mean that the mechanical thrum of our technology is almost totally absent. All the noises are natural—wind moving the brilliant marsh grass and a hysterical dog in the distance. The grass is growing between the boards in the grange steps. A bee hovers, its wings, speeded to invisibility, holding its fat body in the air, built to sweet purpose, like only the rarest of man's machines.

All this is jarred by a plastic six-pack container in the grass and a car speeding by, laughter, something shouted. Could I be a strange sight, a middle-aged man sitting alone on the grange hall steps, eating lunch and basking? Or is it just pack-generated laughter called forth in some of our young by anything out of rote?

But there is something not quite real here. I know what it is! I have been here over an hour and only one boy has come by on a bicycle; no one has passed on his own two feet. So that's what is askew. There is no one walking in the village, a village that was built in a time of walking. If you did not walk you rode or were pulled by a horse. It was an age geared to a different time quantum. Transportation certainly determines our use of the time and our attitude toward it. Could our alienation from earth be so profound because we are machine propelled instead of foot propelled? Man's perception of nature is in inverse proportion to his speed.

But it is easy to romanticize our walking, horse-and-buggy days. A trip on a bitter Maine winter day by horse and buggy could be a frozen hell. It was almost better to walk and keep the blood of the extremities heated. I remember walking in the cutting wind until cheek and mouth stiffened to icy pain, only to be partly rewarded by the thaw over hot cocoa in a warm kitchen full of cooking smells. In the summer there was the nuisance of horse flies, in the spring of black flies, miseries with no ready escape into a car. Antibiotics and modern medicine were missing. O the raging infections and persistent fevers that often were a hopeless battle by antibodies unassisted by man's discovery of nature set against nature (mold against bacteria); and do not forget the freezing run to the frozen seat of the out-house. Blessings upon the best of modern medicine, plumbing, and hi-fi!

Then the roads were laced with manure, flyspecked but sweet smelling stuff in comparison with our internal combustion machine and its acrid exudate of aromatic hydrocarbons, oxides of nitrogen, and lead. Manure is pure weighted against the deadly clouding of our air by exhaust. Furthermore, a horse sometimes didn't listen, but a car never does. And the horse became a member of the family, a real, live, warm one.

Of course we can't go back. Perhaps at best we can only be determined to solve the problems our use of machines has posed for us and to keep expanding our use of horses, bicycles and legs.

Despite the diversions, I hope I have made it plain why I will not tell where my nineteenth-century Maine village is. If a hundred people know of it and tell no one and they don't all visit on the same day, all will be well. But if thousands know and tell thousands our little village will become choked with automobiles, pizza parlors, ice-cream stands, and gas stations to keep pace with the people. More means less. Finally, where once the village stood there will be a plastic monument saying, "This was the site of a perfect example of a nineteenth-century Maine village."

That is the law of diminishing returns.

Girl and horse

Reflections on Pemaquid Point

In an age when fifteen cents buys almost nothing, it does still allow you to park your car above that spit of Maine called Pemaquid Point: a wild collection of blue, green, gray-to-orange rock ledges left by the receding ice age: a sea rock garden filled with natural design and smoothed by the cold pulse of the sea, all presided over by a whitewashed granite block lighthouse.

What an abundant smile greets one at the toll gate! It is light years away from the chill impersonality of that nonseeing hand mechanically sliding tokens to "whoever you are," out of the dark underground cubicle of a subway booth. A smile that sets up the right mood for the visit; and if no pain, physical or mental, is pressing, and you do bother to get out of the car and wander down the rock slopes toward the sea, you will realize that fifteen cents is a most modest toll for this particular Maine experience.

Sit on a contorted rock, bask in the sun, watch and listen to the sea working on America, and follow the takeoff, flight, and landing of the ever-adaptable gulls, full of the hungry grace of life. Breathe that sharply pure air, tinged only with the smell of seaweed and a hint of decaying fish; a primal current is set up between you and that overwhelming uterine broth that created and sustains us all.

Is this sense of connection to the sea happening to the other people scattered on the rocks, some alone, some couples and a few small family groups, all having settled into positions that somehow maintain enough space to give a sense of privacy? How good: enough room for the not too many.

On this lovely gentle day, with the sea showing not a trace of the harshness that can make us fear and curse it, this feeling of primal connection can infuse the mind, pushing into the subliminal all those frantic gropings and distractions, those thousands of busy movements we make in order to function in the world we

10

V.F.W. Post, Norridgewock

have made for ourselves. Perhaps here today on Pemaquid Point we can, for a moment, observe ourselves being a part of nature. This mood is expressed with exquisite rightness by Jorge Guellén in "Perfection" from his Cántico:

> *Curved, the firmament remains*
> *Densely blue, above the sky.*
> *It moves toward that encircling*
> *Of magnificence: midday.*
> *All is a dome. Quietly*
> *There at the center rests the rose,*
> *Subject of the noonday sun.*
> *And so much does the moment lend*
> *That the traveling foot can feel*
> *The completeness of the planet.*

Is this why the sea can have such a grip on the sailor? Is the daily chance for the purification of sea watching the actual magnet? But do real men, working on real ships (miles of metal to paint, close-quartered, breathing hot oil fumes, living in their tightly organized world of throbbing machinery), feel this evocative power of the sea to connect them to the universe? I like to think so. It may not be articulate, but this power must be there in the quieter moments between watches, so "That the traveling foot can feel the completeness of the planet." What else keeps them so long, womanless, in a world often of heaving, heat-baked, or glacial misery? Does this world they live in lighten the pressures generated by the seeming uncontrollability of events on the mainland? Despite the bane and blessing of modern communications, could their sky- and sea-encapsulated home still be remote and insulated enough so that the constant flare-up of social disruption in the densely packed, landbound world does

Farm buildings

not erode their enjoyment of just living,
as it can so insidiously for the land-
lubber? Who will do a psychological
study of the life-style, the satisfactions
and discontents of captains, mates,
engineers, seamen, deckhands, wipers,
and all those who stick with the sea,
who even when they leave it for a while
seem to be irresistibly drawn back?
Maybe we ought to know why men
spend their lives at sea; it might even
teach us more important things than
the study of the cold sterile moon, now
partly stripped of its romance.

I know psychological studies are
often suspect, sometimes rightly so, for
they can certainly be simplistic, mechanical, inhuman, wrong-goaled, or down-
right silly. But concentrated attention to
individual and social psychology focused
with empathy and philosophical ampli-
tude could be a real "giant step for mankind." Such a focus could begin to show
us what we have become and where
we are today. Imagine a transformation
of our gee-whiz rocket-ejaculation,
big-bang power into a far more valid con-
struct for our national pride: the effort
to study and begin to understand the
interior of our collective and individual
psyches. Are not most of the projects
we are spending heavy money on

distractions that seem to pull us ever farther from the real problems on our backs? To avoid immediate alienation of the scientific community, let me emphasize that I think a psychological study in a vacuum is a dumb experiment, usually with sterile results. It must certainly be melded with sociology, biology, anthropology, physiology, and ecology, along with a hard look at our massive diseconomies. But all such effort may not be worth a damn if not fused with art, music, poetry, theater, and love.

Conceivably such a massive probe into what we want may reveal that ever more suburbia, ever larger shopping centers, ever more goods, ever more extraction from the earth until it all runs out, is our concept of the good life that we are determined to accomplish. In which case the whole study project will have been eminently worth while, for it will have given me fair warning to go to sea.

So back to the sailor, this time to the man, or woman, who goes to sea; not for livelihood, but for selflihood, and especially the sailor who is under canvas. Yes, I know something about him. I know his connection to the earth is as primal as a bird in flight and his sails are his wings. The love and sweat and tears he lavishes on his boat could make the most beautiful women envious. Why shouldn't he dote on it so? That marvelous, ancient invention is his ticket to nirvana!

Pemaquid Point is a ship at sea. Without the slightest danger of seasickness, its mood generates, as you can see, thoughts of sailing ships, sea, earth, life past and present; and if you should feel it is all too perfect, there is a touch of the real world just beyond the high water mark in the spoor of homo wastensis: broken bottles, beer and pop cans, and shed Polaroid skins.

Will people always remain incurably oblivious to the visual affront of their inorganic droppings? My universal mood of benign tolerance generated by the timeless rocks and ledges of

Pemaquid Point is being undercut by that mold of mind holding the view that nature's open space was created as one vast personal receptacle for human effluvia. Those who love the American land must become more and more beset with a nostalgia for the older harmonies of nature with man, before he began to overwhelm so much of her with technological waste, both in its deeper and more poisonous forms as well as in the mountains of conspicuous trivia he has built.

Not that there are no new harmonies; we have those, but only as oases in the vast esthetically numbing sprawls we have been generating for so long. Grist for the mill of painters, sculptors, composers, and photographers are the beauties within the general deterioration. This is as it should be. But all the while there is the background radiation of a sadness while the exploration goes on. At the same time there is the feeling of the durability of nature, even if man manages to see to it that he will no longer be included in her schemes. There is also the hope of an eventual realization of the symbiotic tie between technological man and nature in the concerned voices now being heard, and the lovely harmonies with nature that have been created. This leaves open the possibility that man may still achieve a harmonious overall balance and steady recycling state with nature. This must, by necessity, be man's ultimate goal, and the preoccupation of the arts will be not the colorful throes of the final loss, but an ever increasing awareness of the beauty of the earthly processes as revealed by human consciousness.

Yes, do visit Pemaquid Point. It will give you a sense of the durability of earth and sea. It will show artful nature at work with her basic medium, rock. It will be restful, and hopefully it will make you thoughtful; then you will know that the Point, despite its enormous solidity, is far more fragile than you had ever suspected.

Pool, Cliff House, Ogunquit

From the Camden Hills

Moss, Pleasant Point

Cabin, Glen Cove

Of Lighthouses and Keepers

Is the granite or brick solidity of a Maine lighthouse symbolic, representing what man is capable of erecting for permanence, instead of for the fast deal? Is not the startling purity of a whitewashed lighthouse also a symbol of the best in his altruism? This is architecture stoutly formed and conscientiously maintained to help mankind avoid running aground, whether through bad luck, misinformation, or just plain dumbheadedness. After immersing myself in the history of the lighthouse service I find that the image of high purpose and devotion to duty remains essentially untarnished. It is in the course of devious human nature, though, that even the best of projects can generate opposition.

Lighthouses were the last things wanted by the wreckers (sometimes known as "moon cussers" because they cursed the moon when it lit the way for coastal shipping), and they savagely fought any such guardian or rescue system, in their own territories at any rate.

Looking at lighthouses, often in the dramatic setting of sea-swept islets and craggy promontories, one wonders about the life-style of their keepers, in the earlier days before the Coast Guard took over and lighthouse keeping ceased to be a family enterprise. The traditional image is that lighthouses were run by men of crusty, hermitlike mien; loners who fitted into the isolation and self-sufficiency of the keeper's world, perhaps having that lean of mind which liked the uninterrupted thought that solitude could give them. Even Albert Einstein indulged in this romantic notion when he said, "I notice how the monotony of a quiet life stimulates the creative mind. Certain callings in our modern organization entail such an isolated life. I think of occupations such as service in the lighthouse. Would it not be possible to fill such places with young people who wish to think out

Freeport *Wiscasset*

Churchyard   *Belgrade Lakes*

Antique Shop. Woolwich

Stonington

32   *Seal Cove*

Truck. Bath

New Sharon

38   *Lobster Bait*

problems?" Although there are no doubt at isolated stations periods of calm that allow one to think outside the daily stream of self and light maintenance, the steady uninterrupted peace the mind requires to build edifices of philosophical or scientific thought comes just as hard, if not much harder, to the keeper of a lighthouse as it comes to the rest of us. Certainly in the days before modern electronics, it came much harder.

The world of the lighthouse keeper fifty to a hundred and fifty years ago is the one I think of when I look at a lighthouse: the eternal lens cleaning, clockwork-machinery cleaning and lubrication, the wick trimming, the building maintenance — this last exacerbated in Maine by some of the harshest winter weather conditions imaginable — the ice chipping, the water hauling, the boiler firing for steam to drive the foghorns. Add to this the unforeseen storm damage and emergency rescues and it is evident that conditions were hardly conducive for the keeper to be absorbed in the contemplative or creative life. Yet, aside from thinking about the hard practical and personal problems, there is no doubt an easy, drifting, comfortable activity of the mind that goes with routine work, a process that keeps one sane: the binding of life to the fulfillment of duty.

The dream of living the complete life, with time to develop our creative spirit, is always with us. George R. Putnam, former commissioner of the lighthouse service and a most enlightened expert civil servant with a deep interest in his profession (would that our government had many more of this breed), cites in his book *Sentinel of the Coasts*, some letters of application that embody beautifully the pursuit of this dream.

A man, living far from salt water, wrote a letter to the President: "I want to be a lighthouse caretaker on one of those islands out at sea. You may think it strange that I so much desire a desolate life, like the one offered a lighthouse caretaker, but

solitude is just what I want and need. I want to make a study of inventions, also to write books and stories. The lighthouse islands are the most suitable for this work. The solitude of the sea is what I want. I am competent to take care of a lighthouse and hope you will assist me in this matter and that I may prove of great service to our great country by inventing items of value."

There was also the woman applicant, evidently a widow, who wanted a position as keeper of a lighthouse: "I don't want it where it is hot, or where it is fierce storms of bitter cold, but where I could let my youngest girl go to school, where there are certain refinements and nice families for her to know as a growing girl. I want the position for the rest of my life as I can't afford to move from place to place and I get attached to things. I also write stories occasionally for the magazines and papers and would like this kind of life, as quiet is necessary to succeed at that. If you had a bit of grass where we could have a garden, some chickens, and a cow I feel we would give you the most help; hope there are lobsters and good fishing, but please, no sharks!"

These two letters are somehow deeply moving to me because they say—both on the male and the female side—what so many of us want, with the direct simplicity of a touching innocence.

The widow's letter does connect to a reality here, though not exactly in such a lovely dream fulfillment. Many women were in complete charge of our lighthouses, and they were mostly widows, although they were daughters, aunts, and spinsters as well. In fact, in the old days before the Coast Guard took over, the world of the lighthouse was literally held together by women. The urgency of women's importance is highlighted in a wonderfully macabre way by the tale of the keeper of a remote island light who rowed the body of his dead spouse through a turbulent sea to the mainland. There he replaced her with a brand-new wife and rowed right back home, for the beacon must not be left untended even for one night. This must be the most hardheaded, practical swap ever!

Keepers of the lights were man-and-wife teams in a very vital sense. Most wives had to learn how to run the lighthouse-signal system, for in the event of the illness or absence of the keeper fetching supplies his wife was the only one available to keep things functioning, though sometimes the children, if old enough, could serve. And of course the written and unwritten law was that the light or fog system must not cease or there would be inevitable disaster. Shipping traffic on the Maine coast in the nineteenth century was heavy indeed, with enormous cargoes of ice, lumber, granite, coal, and farming appliances, as well as passengers. Steamers plied the coast between Portland and North Yarmouth, and Europe had direct connections to Portland. In the event of a keeper's demise the wife very often took over, sometimes on a temporary basis until a replacement could be found but often permanently, out of cruel necessity, as pensions for widows or keepers—even those with forty to fifty years of service—were nonexistent. The mean-spirited Congress did not vote a pension for keepers until 1918. Women lighthouse keepers were as great in their devotion to duty as any men keepers, and their competence was self-evident; many of them stayed on the job for decades. In the early 1850's the records show thirty women keepers in service.

Lighthouse keeping was often a family enterprise, sometimes a very large one. There was a Maine keeper with as many as seventeen children, so *all* his time was not spent in just polishing his lighthouse equipment. Often the lighthouse had a small farm attached, as at Pemaquid Point, and so work filled day and night with livestock and soil to attend to as well as the light. The distaff side of the keeper team seemed also to keep her mate in

44

Ogunquit shore

Two ladies, York

47

line if he inclined toward sloppiness, as so many of us males do. The inspectors who made the rounds of lighthouses knew that if the living quarters were as neat as a pin, but the light was a bit dingy, a compliment to the wife and a hint to her about the condition of the lighthouse would insure that the husband would be on the neat and narrow by the next inspection.

Most women — dear creatures, some — can make a pleasant home anywhere. I am thinking of that ocean-swept five-acre island, Mount Desert Rock, twenty-six miles at sea, where in wild weather the seas drive completely over it with a force that can move boulders weighing seventy-five tons. In calmer weather, during the spring and summer, as many bushels of soil as possible were brought out, packed in the clefts of bare rock, and planted with flowers, giving this desolate place a touch of garden color and the feel of being among growing things and satisfying a hunger which when unappeased settles a profound depression upon the psyche. Of course the winter gales swept all the results of this painstaking nurture back into the sea, but the need to cultivate one's garden would start the cycle again next spring. Curiously enough the tenders that supply the offshore stations with food, building materials, mail, fuel, and relief men, and that must land all these critical supplies in the dirtiest of weather on most unhospitable shores, have names like *Iris*, *Goldenrod*, *Dandelion*, *Geranium*, and *Heliotrope*. Such incongruity is charming.

Many of the keepers were certainly cast in the heroic mold. Of the women keepers there is the saga of Abbie Burgess, daughter of a Captain Burgess, who by the age of seventeen could run the light and fog system at Matinicus Island, another sea-lashed post twenty-five miles from the mainland. One time when her father had sailed to Rockland for supplies but was bound to the mainland by four weeks of unremitting storms, Abbie, completely on her own, took care of her sickly mother, her sister, and the chickens, and kept the lighthouse functioning. Abbie Burgess and lighthouses were meant for each other—she married the son of a lighthouse keeper and spent her life in the service.

As an old lady she wrote in one of her letters: "I think the time is not far distant when I shall climb these lighthouse steps no more. I wonder if care of the lighthouse will follow my soul after it has left this worn out body. If I ever have a gravestone I would like it in the form of a lighthouse or beacon." She died in 1892. New Englanders, who take a little time deliberating over things but who do have long memories, did erect a memorial in the shape of a lighthouse over her grave at Spruce Head in 1945, only fifty-three years after her death.

George Putnam, in citing some remarkable instances of devotion to duty on the part of women lighthouse keepers, tells the story of the keeper of Angel Island Light in San Francisco Bay. She reported that the machinery of the fog signal was disabled on July 2, 1906, and that she had struck the bell by hand for twenty hours and thirty-five minutes, until the fog lifted. (Apparently she was also a most precise time keeper.) On July 4, the machinery was further disabled, so she stood on the outside platform all night and "struck the bell with a nail hammer with all my might."

There is Ida Lewis of the Lime Rock lighthouse, which sits on a ledge in Newport Harbor. She lived there for fifty-seven years, was official keeper of the light for thirty-two years, and saved thirteen persons and one sheep from drowning. Indeed the saga of lighthouses that ring the coasts of the world is filled with an aura of incredible devotion to duty and jobs to be done, all with a remarkable amount of self-discipline and sacrifice—effort expended in the saving of human life, instead of *duty* used as a shibboleth for the destructive acts we perform against man and nature.

*Young farmer
and steer*

Manure cart

Rock, Ogunquit   *Gravestone, Bowditch*

Signs, Woolwich

Farmhouse door

Miller

Lobsterman

Abandoned farm

Near Rome

Yes, there were lapses in discipline, and certainly enough examples of sloppiness and carelessness, but all were so quickly revealed when the lights went out and the horns failed to blow that dereliction of duty was never a long-term process. There was, too, the nasty game of political appointing of keepers. A new appointee could arrive, as unannounced as the fates, knock on the door of the lighthouse with his letter of appointment in hand, and take over. This abuse was fortunately replaced by a strict merit system within the civil service. There were also the lack of pensions, the low pay, and the strained relations resulting from being in close quarters for months at a time, so that the sound of the other keeper slurping his soup was enough to drive one to murder, though there does not seem to be a record of any. Perhaps keepers were kept so busy that a real homicidal pathology did not develop, though they would go about their duties not speaking to each other for weeks at a time.

Man is a strange duty-bound creature, which can be a blessing when the duty is joined with expertise to attain a moral goal, such as involvement in a system designed to forestall disaster. Maintenance of lighthouses, whether by a family unit or by a loner or, as at present, by the Coast Guard administration, is, in a total view, one of man's brighter chapters.

When all our coasts are guarded by automatic mechanisms run by electronics, we will surely miss the companionable sweep of the beacon across the darkening sea. Though I will not miss, at close quarters anyway, the latest efficiency of the fog siren such as the one I had to bear for two days on Monhegan Island. This monster had the penetrating rasp that scraped the nerves raw and generated a profound hatred on the part of all the residents —a clear case of efficiency designed without regard for those who might have to live with it. Long stay dead the SST!

No doubt in the very near future all lighthouses will be

Boathouse, Camden

run by the modern technology of radio beam and radar, all automatic. As this technology is directed toward the conservation of life, sad as it will be to see the lights go out, I will welcome the new efficiency harnessed to this purpose. But please never tear down those wonderful architectural symbols filled with memories of harsh and pleasant duty; those clean forms set in untamed nature and filled with beautifully balanced clockwork in shining brass, whose purpose was to revolve the light that guided us. We demolish too much of our past that has beauty in its design, history, and intent.

Camp handyman   Back hoe driver   *Aroostook roadside*

A Nose for Maine

If your smeller is in good order and has not been paralyzed by the masochism of tobacco or the assaults of urban noxmiasmas, Maine is bound to open a new world of scent for you. Moreover, it might give you insight into the nose-controlled universe of the wild creature where the urgent messages of the malodorous and redolent, carried on each breeze, determine his every move.

What a pity our olfactory perception has diminished so greatly in its power to carry signals of the fragrant. But ever more vital, the alarums broadcast in our mephitic age may go unheeded because that clogged remnant we call a nose, having lost the ability to drive into our brain piercingly enough the messages, "stay away from it," "get rid of it," no longer can fulfill its proper function as a protective mechanism.

O dog, twitching in your dream chase, on the next trip to

Pemaquid ledges

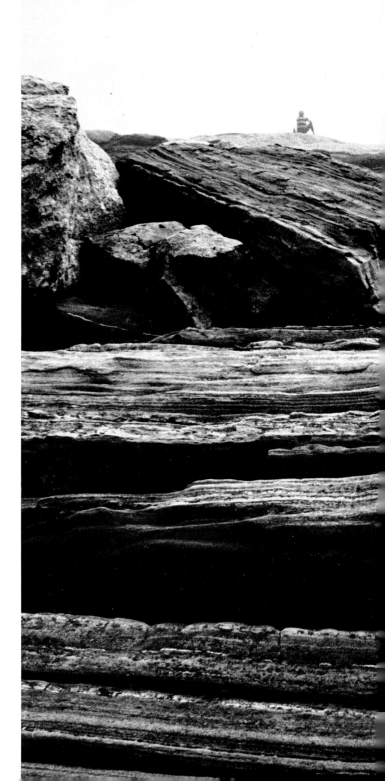

Maine you should be with me and left to run wild in the meadows and woods so that all the timeless messages generated by nature can blow your mind! What pleasure to watch your joy and excitement as your nose skims the earth.

After a lovely stay in the outback of Maine, standing in the middle of Boston on a hot, hazed-over July afternoon, trying to keep the breathing shallow in the traffic fumes, I ask my city-bred companion, "How can you stand the stink?" The reply is, "What stink?" Poor mankind, where have your dog days gone?

But certainly all is not lost; that is, if you have not totally brutalized your osmotic membrane. Do come and meet a summer morning with it in that time when the dew is still being burned off and islands of fog still hug the hollows and hang over the lakes. Move yourself through this morning on your own two feet, or a bicycle, or do at least stop your car, shut off the engine and just keep still. You will bathe in the fragrance of the grasses, weeds, wildflowers, and the earth of Maine, and you will know what a sweet factory nature is, to make the world young again every morning. Yet for the early morning wanderer this is only the beginning; by his nose he will be led into the smell of cow manure, the smell of hay, the smell of wood smoke, and be all enveloped in that early summer tropical lushness, a fantastic richness of moss, ferns, and water plants.

That all this opulence, held in perfect profile in the secret deep freeze of a Maine winter, blossoms into such aromatic fecundity is incredible, especially with the remembrance of having stood in almost this exact spot last winter, when it was a bleak snow-swept hillside in an apparently lifeless world.

Perfumed Maine, blessed with that vast Canadian bellows rhythmically pumping you full of sharp pure air, what a treat you

Toll house keeper, Pemaquid Point

are for the abused nose and sooty lung. May you find the strength to keep at bay the ever encroaching fetid vapor seeping in from the south of you. May you find the will to clean up your pockets of rotten cabbage stink that surround your pulp factories, and the kerosene reek of oil spills. Any "progress" that asks you to sell your birthright of sweet air to breathe should be taken and buried like the evil-smelling thing it is.

But, far from such depressing airs, I know where there is an old-fashioned swimming hole, fed by a stream, clear, cold, and uncontaminated. A pool that morning becomes like no other time of day: the early sun patterns its surface and the deep pockets of shadow open up. Swallows skim the water in their endless graceful sweep for insects, programmed by a million years of evolution to this perfection of flight and hunt. Apart from the bird cries, there is profound silence, overlaid by the smell of river mud and watercress. Here I float looking through the trees that canopy this retreat, at a sky washed so fresh and new that the very thought of mucking it up is painfully obscene and quite beyond comprehension. The chill of such thoughts meets the chill of a cooling body, but a brisk swim shatters the silence and returns warmth and optimism. What a glorious way to start the day, this Nordic toning of the body. The Scandina-

Pemaquid rocks

vians have a truth in their ritual of the steam bath and the dash into the snow. It must either shake one into pulsing life, or out of it! But this is summer, and though winter has not quite left the pool yet, the delight of this morning swim in Eden is really only harsh in the initial plunge. After such a swim and commune with nature there is just the right end to a perfect day's beginning: a rough towel rubdown standing in the aroma of sunlit pine needles, then to the cabin, led by the smell of frying bacon, to sate the morning hunger with a hot breakfast bought in the supermarket and cooked on a modern stove. The technology of civilization is very nice, too, kept in proper perspective and harnessed to nature's, and therefore my, well-being.

So prepare your nose for Maine and let no cigarettes interfere with the experience. This method of desensitization, which no doubt is a form of protection against the urban reek of megalopolis, will not be necessary here. Get off the busy roads; they also are killers of the sweet air and bury all that is delicate and fragrant in exhaust and the shriek of speed. Park and walk on the quiet back roads, or just park, if that is your wont. In the biting season, don't forget the insect repellent. Nature decrees that all things must feed, but it need not be on you.

Get up early. Yes, I know bed is very nice, especially curled up with another companionable body, but the occasional sacrifice of an early rising brings reward out of all proportion to the effort. Ask the angler: does he get up for the fish alone, or is the angling partly an excuse to catch the early morning?

Surrounded by the essence of morning in Maine, you will quickly understand the axiom "The nose knows how the world goes."

Nubble Light　　　　*Deer Isle*

From Littlefield's Village   *Coastal Inlet*

Frenchman Bay   *Near Cushing*   79

Cape Rosier, Penobscot Bay   *Palmyra*

Corn Field

Barn   *Cape Elizabeth Light*

*Ice Patterns
at Prout's Neck*

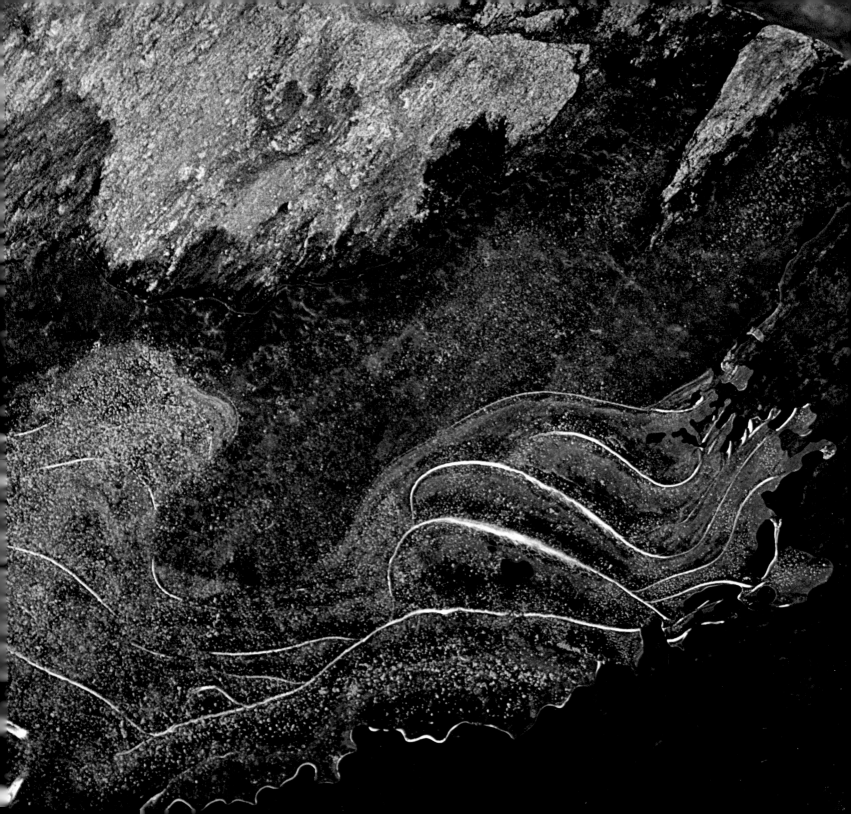

Of Livelihood

Is Maine one of the last American bulkwarks against the tide of routinization and cubbyholing of man's work? Mass production, though certainly here in paper, pulp, leather, and textile industries, does not seem to have completely overwhelmed the granite integrity of a basic way of life that has for so long been rooted in the harvesting of the land and sea.

In this state whose size can almost swallow the rest of New England but which is populated by little more than a million people, there is a marvelous spaciousness inherent in the living and working environment. Even in the cities, because the wilderness and country are within easy reach, there is a feeling quite remote from the pressure-cooker tensions of so much of the Eastern United States. Much of Maine's smaller community life is quite parochial, perhaps, but it is also a life with some of the certainties left. Most of all, and best of all, Maine still nourishes the true small entrepreneur, who pursues a way of life that seems to be rapidly drying up in the rest of our country, where that inexorable drive toward systems of mass production is bending our very souls to its methodology.

Do not misconstrue. I am not a Luddite. Mass production is a necessity in this technological, mass-populated civilization of ours. (Otherwise it is most unlikely that you would be holding this book in your hands.) But if, as studies show, 16 to 50 per cent of nonprofessional workers in our country are unhappy with their jobs—jobs that take up half of their waking hours or more—something is very seriously askew. Here may well be the root of many of our modern distempers and discontents. Alienation from our work, so much of which has

A fresh coated ship
　Warm in the sun
Waiting to have its mast winged
　And meet the cool blue sea.

Not a machine stamped thing
　Drawing the gulls' cry
Into the hot sound
　Of internal combustion.

Moving to a more elemental tune
　Of the sea's rill against planking
And the wind strum
　Of taut sheeting.

All sung in perfect ecology
　The morning air arrives
And moves man's lovely contrivance;
　Then leaves unchanged,
Soon smoothed
　In the vast atmospheric sea.

lost any sense of self-direction toward goals of creative usefulness, is the stigma of our time. In the last analysis the cornucopia of badly designed, sloppy, or even dangerous consumer goods punched out by a mass-production system could be laying waste our psyches as well as the natural world, and will prove to be no more than a Barmecidal banquet.

Maine is still a land with many occupations in which the pacing of self is possible and where the sense of building a destiny of your own can be realized. This allows a choosing of your own time and direction; a gamble that gives meaning and spice to one's life work, provided that society is so set up that it does not let you go down the drain, should you fail completely.

Take that symbol of rugged independence, the lobster-man, not as a quaint, over-romanticized figure but as he really is. Though he is tied to the weather, his traps, the fluctuations of the catch, and the ever increasing chance that one of man's uncontrolled commercial activities could have disastrous effects on the breeding grounds of the crustacean harvest, basically he is freer than most of us. There are certainly the problems of building, buying, and maintaining such capital equipment as boat, traps, markers, winches, ropes, wharf space, and storage; work often set in cold, raw, hard conditions. Even though anxieties plague the lobsterman, just like the rest of us, the difference in the meaning of his work life and the work life of an assembly-line worker in Detroit is of the profoundest nature. The lobsterman fits himself to his job: he sees the direct results of his skill and workmanship as a personal achievement. The aching of his back is of his own choosing, and the daily details of his work are not locked

Dairy farmer

in the predictability of rote. How fine it is to watch his
unconscious skill as he handles his boat and moves in the open
in a natural world akin to that of the hunter, and where the
active life tends to keep him fit. A lobsterman I talked with
had learned his skills as a lad, when he started going out every
day with his father, and had continued in his craft all of his
life, a flow of work satisfaction broken only by a spell in the
trenches and mud of France during World War I. Now well over
seventy, he still tends his traps every day, though admitting
that sometimes his rheumatism does bother him just a bit. The
daily catch he brings in is paid for cash in hand, and there is
very little paperwork, though no doubt that is increasing with
our proliferating bureaucracy. His position has respect and
status, the value of which, to my mind, simply cannot be
overestimated.

This positioning in a work hierarchy, and its importance,
was very directly expressed by a young fellow I spoke with who
was truck-hauling lobster bait, and who very soon got around
to letting me know that this was only a temporary job. He had
been south, meaning somewhere below Maine, but did not like it
much and wanted to return to his home state. In order to make that
possible he had taken this job, but only for the moment, you
understand, while waiting for an opening as a telephone lineman.
This would be a position with status and some manly charisma
set within the movement and variety of different daily work
problems. It has always been amazing to me what a hard,
dangerous, dirty job a man will do, with positive enthusiasm,
provided it has an aura of free-ranging machismo and respect.

Look at the life of the lumberjack. Even though lived in
the framework of large corporations—the big paper and pulp

Barn and field, Aroostook

companies—his is very much the life of the cowboy, that other figure of rugged American independence. The lumberjack lives in a camp and bunkhouse outpost somewhere deep in those sixteen million acres of woods, cutting and herding trees through the fall and winter, when the insect life doesn't swarm, and operating pretty much on his own as long as he gets the job done. His existence has a harsh, slightly monastic quality; without drinking or women in camp (at least that is a strict company rule), his leisure time is spent mostly in card playing, television watching, talking, or reading. His life is in fact a partial return to earlier frontier simplicities, with a sense of being somewhat of a maverick and of doing something difficult.

How about the Maine farmer? Perhaps he is not quite as free ranging a spirit as the lobsterman, rooted as he is to his acreage, but still he lives in a landscape formed and nurtured by his own efforts, and can see the palpable results of them. I talked to a dairy farmer in Aroostook who had formerly been in potatoes, but now, despite the daily urgency of emptying his cows, preferred dairy farming to potato farming, because, as he put it, dairy farming was a way to go broke more slowly. Over seventy years old, he had just come out of the hospital the previous week. While he talked to me it was obvious that getting enough air to

Grange Hall

his lungs was an effort. I asked if it was emphysema that had compelled his visit to the hospital. "Yep. It's my punishment for smoking anything that would burn, for forty years."

As we stood, on this rainy spring day, chatting in front of his huge and rather magnificent barn, which was attached to a fine specimen of a Maine farmhouse, I was saddened by the thought of what might become of this family homestead, built with loving skill, maintained by generations of hard work, and which had become a monument to man's care of the earth. Here was a farmer who only managed to hang on to his property because his son was able to take leave from his city job and help out. The old man's wife had died two years before, and the children were away living their own lives. There really seemed to be no one to carry on. What would happen to the big old place? It obviously could not be run by a retired couple.

I have seen many farms in Maine deserted and falling down. Would that be the fate of this one? Would it have the luck to be bought by some family whose livelihood did not depend on proximity to urban life and who could and would afford to maintain it? Would the land be subdivided, and its history wiped out? Or would it become the extension of another farm? Was it folly to hope that the land might continue to be cultivated, and that this grand barn and house would be saved?

How reassuring that not all the young want to leave the farms. At one place where I stopped to take a picture I spoke with a young man who was going to carry on the family tradition, and who was obviously already absorbed in raising steers for beef. He beamed with great satisfaction as he showed me his solidly packed animals, prime enough to gladden the heart of any butcher. There seems to be somewhat of a reversal of the

Wharf, Stonington

In a few places
houses can still stand
isolated
not sweated into
niggardly plots,
existing in
a dignity of aloneness
allowing the landscape
to be perceived.

In a few places
people can still stand
isolated
not sweated into
niggardly bureaucracies,
existing in
a dignity of aloneness
allowing the soul
to be perceived.

Field near Boothbay

farmboy exodus to the city. Quite a few young people are staying on the land, to lead a life that, despite its problems, is less abrasive. Yes, a smaller community, though knowing too much about you, may be better than the anonymity of modern urban life, where everyone knows and cares too little about you.

The chips in the gamble of potatoes in Aroostook County are the Kennebecs, the Katahdins, the Cherokees, and the Chippewas — potatoes labeled with Indian memories, and cultivated in the endless combed plains of Aroostook. The blights of monoculture, the gambling-casino atmosphere of the fluctuating potato market are risks that the Aroostook farmer has learned to live with, and in the years when you don't make it big you can always eat the potatoes. The potato is apparently a crop well suited to the short growing season and the bitter winter here, because it can be stored in barns that are half-buried in the ground and thereby kept from freezing. Picking potatoes seems to be very much a community business,

Long Pond, Belgrade Lakes

Farmhouse near Bristol   Coffee stand, Bucksport   107

Duck

Cape Elizabeth

SOUTH
CONGREGATIONAL
CHURCH
Rev. Robert M. Howes
Parsonage: North St.
MORNING WORSHIP 11 A.M.
CHURCH ORGANIZED 1790
The Building Erected 1824

except of course on the farms with large enough acreage to use the mechanical harvester. In the six-week harvesting season everyone is out in the fields, children included, looking like commas scattered in a midwestern plain.

So much of the harvesting of Maine's bounty is a family business, seasonal work that brings in cash to carry through the long winter, or for extras to make life more pleasant. There is blueberry picking in the vast barrens of Washington County, the making of Christmas wreaths around the kitchen tables, with the fragrance of spruce and gossip intermingled. The whistle at the sardine cannery signals a catch coming in, and all those women on permanent call drop everything—well almost everything —to get on the packing line, their nimble fingers inserting silver fish into silver tins. There is the seasonal catering to that other economic asset of vast importance, the tourists, who come in great schools of shining cars to enjoy the coves, harbors, islands, beaches, lakes, parks, historic sights, hunting, fishing, and antiquing. This is a seasonal swarming over the land that is, like so many things, a mixed blessing, creating along with profits, a commercialism that swamps a past which depends for its beauty and interest upon reasonable use of its dimension, and change not inimical to its basic design.

Maine, may you preserve as much as possible of your ancient mode of culturing the sea and the land, and prosper in it, and not be misled by the blandishments of the assembly line, whether it is popping out rivets or tourists. A banner dating from the China trade hangs in the Searsport museum and is embroidered with the legend KINDNESS TO PASSENGERS BE CELEBRATED. Let me paraphrase this into "kindness to the land be celebrated," as befits a state whose seal depicts a farmer, a sailor, a pine tree, and a moose.

First Congregational Church, Kennebunkport

Owl's Head